OXFORD PUBLIC LIBRARY
213 Choccolocco Street
Oxford, Alabama 36203

The Drug-Alert Dictionary and Resource Guide

The Drug-Alert Dictionary and Resource Guide

A Drug-Alert Book

Jeffrey Shulman

TWENTY-FIRST CENTURY BOOKS
FREDERICK, MARYLAND

Published by
Twenty-First Century Books
38 South Market Street
Frederick, Maryland 21701

Text Copyright © 1991
Twenty-First Century Books

Cover Illustration by David Neuhaus

All rights reserved. No part of this book may be reproduced or utilized in any form or by any means, electronic or mechanical, including photocopying, recording, or by any information storage and retrieval system, without written permission from Twenty-First Century Books.

Printed in the United States of America

10 9 8 7 6 5 4 3 2 1

Library of Congress Cataloging in Publication Data
Shulman, Jeffrey
The Drug-Alert Dictionary and Resource Guide
(A Drug-Alert Book)
Summary: Alphabetically arranged entries introduce drug-related terms, concepts, and issues. A resource guide lists drug-related programs and activities.
1. Drug abuse—Handbooks, manuals, etc.—Juvenile literature.
2. Drug abuse—Information services—United States—Directories—Juvenile literature.
[1. Drug abuse—Dictionaries.
2. Drug abuse—Directories.]
I. Title.
II. Series: The Drug-Alert Series.
HV5801.S464   1991
362.29'03—dc20   90-46534 CIP AC
ISBN 0-941477-85-1

Table of Contents

Introduction 6

Dictionary 9

Resource Guide 65

    Hotlines 66

    Private Agencies 67

    State Government Agencies 70

    Federal Government Agencies 88

    Drug-Free Schools & Communities
       Regional Centers 90

    Canadian Resources 91

Introduction

"Baby Saved by Miracle Drug!" "Drug Bust at Local School!" Headlines like these are often side by side in your newspaper, or you may hear them on the evening news. This is confusing. If drugs save lives, why are people arrested for having and selling them?

The word "drug" is part of the confusion. It is a word with many meanings. The drug that saves a baby's life is also called a medicine. The illegal drugs found at the local school have many names—names like pot, speed, and crack. But one name for all of these illegal drugs is dope.

Some medicines you can buy at your local drugstore or grocery store, and there are other medicines only a doctor can get for you. But whether you buy them yourself or need a doctor to order them for you, medicines are made to get you healthy when you are sick.

Dope is not for sale in any store. You can't get it from a doctor. Dope is bought from someone called a "dealer" or a "pusher" because using, buying, or selling dope is against the law. That doesn't stop some people from using dope. They say they do it to change the way they feel. Often, that means they are trying to run away from their problems. But when the dope wears off, the problems are still there—and they are often worse than before.

There are three drugs we see so often that we sometimes forget they really are drugs. These are alcohol, nicotine, and caffeine. Alcohol is in beer, wine, and liquor. Nicotine is found in cigarettes, cigars, pipe tobacco, and other tobacco products. Caffeine is in coffee, tea, soft drinks, and chocolate. These three drugs are legal. They are sold in stores. But that doesn't mean they are always safe to use. Alcohol and nicotine are such strong drugs that only adults are allowed to buy and use them. And most parents try to keep their children from having too much caffeine.

Marijuana, cocaine, alcohol, nicotine, caffeine, medicines: these are all drugs. All drugs are alike because they change the way our bodies and minds work. But different drugs cause different changes. Some help, and some harm. And when they aren't used properly, even helpful drugs can harm us.

Figuring all this out is not easy. That's why The Drug-Alert Books were written: so you will know why certain drugs are used, how they affect people, why they are dangerous, and what laws there are to control them.

Knowing about drugs is important. It is important to you and to all the people who care about you.

David Friedman, Ph.D.
Consulting Editor

Dr. David Friedman is Associate Professor of Physiology and Pharmacology and Assistant Dean of Research Development at the Bowman Gray School of Medicine, Wake Forest University.

How to Use
The Drug-Alert Dictionary

The Drug-Alert Dictionary is designed to give you a quick overview of some of the most important drug-related terms, concepts, and issues. When appropriate, a dictionary entry indicates other entries where useful information can be found. Notations to see other entries are made in parentheses: for example, *(See: alcohol).*

The dictionary is not intended to replace a more in-depth look at specific drugs. More information on specific drugs and drug-related issues is available in the other volumes of The Drug-Alert Series:

Focus on Drugs and the Brain

Focus on Alcohol

Focus on Marijuana

Focus on Cocaine and Crack

Focus on Nicotine and Caffeine

Focus on Steroids

Focus on Hallucinogens

Focus on Opiates

Focus on Medicines

acid:
a slang term for the hallucinogenic drug LSD. Taking LSD is sometimes called "dropping acid." *(See: hallucinogen, LSD.)*

addict:
a person who is addicted to a drug or drugs. *(See: addiction.)*

addiction:
the constant need or craving for a drug. Certain drugs, called psychoactive drugs, change the way the brain works. *(See: psychoactive drug.)* Addiction means that the use of drugs has changed the brain so much that it begins to need drugs. The addicted brain needs drugs the way the healthy brain needs natural and ordinary pleasures like food and sleep.

The use of addictive drugs disrupts the way the brain controls the senses, movements, thoughts, and emotions. The repeated use of drugs often leads to tolerance, which means that drug users need more of a drug to get the same effect. *(See: tolerance.)* People addicted to drugs depend on them to feel normal and to avoid the painful symptoms of withdrawal. *(See: dependence, withdrawal.)*

Because drug use has changed the way the brain works, addicts feel that they must have drugs. The only thing they care about is getting and using drugs. Drug addiction is a sickness. It is very hard for addicts to stop using drugs by themselves. But they can get better and lead drug-free lives. To recover from drug addiction, a drug addict first needs to admit that he or she does, in fact, have a drug problem and then seek the help of doctors and counselors. *(See: recovery.)*❐

alcohol:

a drug found in beer, wine, and liquor. Alcohol depresses, or slows down, the way the brain works. *(See: depressant.)* It disrupts the messages to and from the brain that control our senses, movements, thoughts, and emotions.

Alcohol enters the bloodstream through the stomach and intestines. When it reaches the brain, alcohol changes the way messages are sent throughout the central nervous system. *(See: psychoactive drug.)* Alcohol disrupts the way the brain receives information from the senses, making it difficult to see and hear clearly. It disrupts the way the brain controls the muscles and body movements. It disrupts the way the brain controls thinking, making it difficult to pay attention, to learn, or to remember things. And it disrupts the way the brain controls the emotions. People who use alcohol may become suddenly sad, angry, or confused. They may feel out of control.

It takes the body about one hour to get rid of one drink of alcohol. When alcohol builds up in the bloodstream, we say that a person is drunk, or intoxicated. When the body is free of alcohol, we say that a person is sober. Many times, people feel sick several hours after they stop drinking alcohol. This sick feeling is called a hangover. *(See: hangover.)*

Alcohol can damage the body. Long-term use can hurt the heart, the liver, the kidneys, the stomach, and the brain. It can cause certain kinds of cancer. It can hurt children before they are born. When a pregnant woman uses alcohol, the drug can cause serious health problems for the unborn child.

Alcohol can also cause long-term changes to the way the brain works. Alcohol is a very addictive drug. *(See: addiction.)* Repeated alcohol use leads to tolerance, or the need for more of a drug to get the same effect, and dependence, or the need to use a drug to avoid withdrawal. *(See: dependence, tolerance, withdrawal.)* Addiction to alcohol is called alcoholism; people who are addicted to alcohol are called alcoholics.

Each year, hundreds of thousands of people get sick or die from diseases due to alcohol. Alcohol use also leads to countless hospital emergencies. One of the worst dangers of alcohol use is when people drink and drive. *(See: DWI.)*

Alcohol is a legal drug for people who have reached the age of 21. But it is against the law for anyone under the age of 21 to buy or use alcohol.◻

Alcohol: Facts and Figures

- There are over 10 million alcoholics in the United States. By 1995, there will be over 11 million.

- Each year, 100,000 people in the United States die from sicknesses due to alcohol. One out of every 20 deaths in the United States is due to alcohol.

- Over 500,000 people enter treatment programs for alcoholism each year.

- The damage caused by alcohol to the economy of the United States is over $100 billion each year.

- 4.6 million teenagers have a drinking problem.

- 5% of high-school seniors drink alcohol every day.

- 93% of high-school seniors have used alcohol.

- Over half of the teenagers who drink started using alcohol before the tenth grade; 10% started before the seventh grade.

- More than one-third of teenagers get drunk once every 2 weeks.

- About one-third of the U.S. population does not drink any alcoholic products.

alcoholic:
a person who is addicted to alcohol. *(See: addiction, alcohol.)*❐

alcoholism:
addiction to alcohol. *(See: addiction, alcohol.)*❐

amotivational syndrome:
the feeling that nothing in life is worth doing. The term "amotivational" means that there is a "lack of motivation," or desire, to do anything. This feeling may develop in people who use a drug or drugs over a long period of time.

People with this problem lose interest in such everyday activities as school, sports, work, and hobbies. They no longer care about what they eat or how they look. They no longer care about their family or their friends. They no longer want to make plans or think about the future. The only thing they care about or want is drugs.❐

amphetamine:
one of several kinds of drugs known as stimulants. Some of the slang terms for amphetamines include speed, pep pills, and uppers. *(See: stimulant.)*❐

anabolic:
See: anabolic steroids.❐

anabolic steroids:

a group of drugs used as a chemical boost or short cut to a more muscular body. Developed in the 1930s, anabolic steroids are a synthetic form of testosterone, the body's male hormone. The term "anabolic" means "tissue-building." Like the natural hormone testosterone, anabolic steroids are used by the body to build up muscle tissue.

Because anabolic steroids are synthetic testosterone, they produce the same kinds of physical changes that the natural male hormone does. In other words, they produce the kind of changes that turn a young boy into a man. Some athletes use anabolic steroids because these drugs help to build up muscles very quickly. And some young people use anabolic steroids because they think that bigger muscles make them look more attractive.

Testosterone is produced naturally by the body, and the production of natural testosterone is very carefully regulated by the testicles, the male sex glands. Using anabolic steroids, however, upsets the body's natural balance of hormones. They produce physical changes that are out of control. Anabolic steroid users may develop thick, shaggy growths of hair on their arms and legs. They may even go bald. They may get very severe cases of pimples.

Other changes are far more dangerous. Using anabolic steroids can damage the heart, liver, and kidneys. It can keep a young person from growing to his or her full height. And male steroid users may lose the ability to father children.

Anabolic steroids do more than damage the body. They can make people moody, easily upset, and highly suspicious of other people. Steroid users may have sudden and violent temper tantrums, often referred to as "roid" rages. Or they may get very depressed and think about killing themselves.

The use of anabolic steroids is a major problem among professional and amateur athletes. Many sports groups have begun to test athletes for the use of anabolic steroids. But the use of steroids is not just a problem for athletes. It is a drug problem for many young people today. It is estimated that as many as one in every 15 high-school seniors has used anabolic steroids. That's 500,000 teenage steroid users.❐

analgesic:

a type of medicine that is used to reduce or stop pain. The term "analgesia" means the "absence of pain." Analgesic medicines include such common household items as aspirin and acetaminophen. These "over-the-counter" pain remedies are bought and used without a doctor's prescription. Much stronger painkillers include narcotic drugs, such as codeine and morphine. *(See: codeine, morphine.)* These drugs are made from opium and are also known as opiates. *(See: opiate.)* They can be bought and used only with a doctor's prescription.❐

anesthetic:
   a medication that causes a loss of feeling, including the sensation of pain. General anesthetics depress, or slow down, the entire central nervous system, causing a person to become unconscious, or to "black out." They are used by doctors when performing major surgery. Local anesthetics block pain signals in only one part of the body from reaching the brain. They are often used during minor surgery and dental procedures.❐

angel dust:
   a slang term for the hallucinogen PCP. Other slang terms for PCP include loveboat, hog, lovely, and killer weed. *(See: hallucinogen, PCP.)*❐

antibiotic:
   a kind of medicine that can stop the growth of harmful germs in the body. Antibiotics are used to treat many different infectious diseases caused by bacteria. *(See: bacteria, germs.)*❐

antibody:
   a natural substance produced by the body's white blood cells to destroy harmful germs. *(See: immune system.)*❐

aspirin:
   one of several drugs known as analgesics. *(See: analgesic.)*❐

BAC:

the abbreviation for "blood alcohol content." The blood alcohol content is the amount of alcohol in a person's body. The BAC may be measured directly by testing a small amount of a person's blood. It can also be measured indirectly by testing a person's breath for traces of alcohol. A special machine called a breathalyzer is used to test the breath.

Police officers often test a person's blood alcohol content to see if he or she has had too much to drink. This is one way that police officers try to keep drunk drivers off the roads. *(See: DWI.)*

bacteria:

a large group of single-celled plants that live everywhere in the world around us. While most bacteria are harmless to the human body (and some are even helpful), there are several kinds of pathogenic, or disease-causing, bacteria.

Disease-causing bacteria, also called pathogens, can carry and pass on infectious diseases from one person to another. Among the diseases caused by such bacteria are whooping cough, tetanus, tuberculosis, scarlet fever, ear infections, strep throat, and diphtheria. *(See: immune system.)*

barbiturate:

one of several kinds of drugs known as depressants. They are commonly referred to as sleeping pills. A slang term for barbiturates is downers. *(See: depressant.)*

beer:

an alcoholic beverage made from several kinds of grains. *(See: alcohol.)*

blood alcohol content:

See: BAC.

blotter:

a special kind of absorbent paper or tissue that is used to hold a dose of the hallucinogenic drug LSD. *(See: hallucinogen, LSD.)*

booze:

a slang term for alcohol and drinks made with alcohol. *(See: alcohol.)*

breathalyzer:

a device that is used to measure a person's blood alcohol content, or BAC, by testing the breath for traces of alcohol. *(See: BAC.)*

caffeine:

a bitter-tasting, odorless drug found in different kinds of plants. The four sources of caffeine are coffee beans, tea leaves, cocoa beans, and cola nuts. From these plants, a wide variety of products containing caffeine are made, including coffee, tea, chocolate, and cola drinks.

Caffeine is a mild stimulant. It speeds up the way the brain and body work. People say that it gives them a boost of energy and makes them more alert. They say it helps them think more clearly and work more quickly. *(See: stimulant.)*

Though it is not as harmful as many other drugs, caffeine is not completely safe. Like other drugs, caffeine can hurt the body. Too much caffeine can cause headaches, diarrhea, and nausea. Like other psychoactive drugs, caffeine changes the way people think, feel, and behave. *(See: psychoactive drug.)* Caffeine can make people very tense or nervous; they feel "on edge." Caffeine is not as addictive as other drugs; but it is habit-forming, and it can be difficult for people to stop using caffeine once they start using it regularly. *(See: addiction.)*

Caffeine is a legal drug, and it is found in many everyday products. Most people do not even think of caffeine as a drug. But it is very easy to get too much of this everyday drug.

Caffeine: How Much Is Too Much?

How much caffeine is too much? Since the effects of caffeine differ from person to person, it is hard to say how much is too much. But many doctors say that an adult should not have more than 250 milligrams of caffeine a day. And young people should have much less than that.

How much caffeine do you use each day? To help you measure how much caffeine you use, here's a chart of some everyday products and the amount of caffeine they contain:

Food or Product:	Caffeine (in milligrams):
Coffee (6 ounces)	
brewed	80-150
instant	40-65
Hot tea (6 ounces)	20-40
Iced tea (12 ounces)	67-76
Soda (12 ounces)	36-54
Chocolate candy (1 ounce)	10-30
Chocolate cake (small slice)	20-30
Chocolate milk (5 ounces)	2-15
Pain relievers (1 tablet)	32-65

cannabis:
the plant from which the drug marijuana comes. The resin of the marijuana plant contains a psychoactive drug called tetrahydrocannabinol, or THC. The leaves and flowering tops of the cannabis plant are dried and then shredded to make the leafy mixture called marijuana. Other words for marijuana are grass and pot. Another word for the marijuana plant is hemp. *(See: marijuana, psychoactive drug.)*❐

COA:
the abbreviation for "children of alcoholics." Alcoholism is often referred to as "the family disease" because it can easily destroy a family. Children are especially hurt when one or both parents suffer from alcoholism. They can't depend on their parents for the care and support that children need. The children of alcoholics often tend to blame themselves for the disruption and distrust that alcoholism brings to the family. They think the problem is their fault. *(See: addiction, alcohol.)*

It is important for the children of alcoholics to realize that they are *not* to blame for the drinking problems of a parent. Alcoholism is a disease, and alcoholics need professional help to recover from their addiction. *(See: recovery.)* The children of alcoholics may need help, too, to cope with the pressures and conflicts that alcoholism causes. Support groups made up of other COAs can offer advice and encouragement.❐

coca:

the plant from which the drug cocaine comes. The coca plant grows wild in the mountainous areas of South America. Coca growers first dry and press the greenish-brown leaves of the coca plant to form a coca paste; then, the coca paste is treated with strong chemicals to make the white, powdery substance known as cocaine. *(See: cocaine.)*

cocaine:

a drug that comes from the leaves of the coca plant. *(See: coca.)* Cocaine is a white mixture that looks like baby powder or powdered sugar. It may be sniffed through the nose or injected into the bloodstream with a hypodermic needle. *(See: hypodermic syringe.)* One form of cocaine, called crack, is made to be smoked. *(See: crack.)*

Cocaine is a stimulant. *(See: stimulant.)* It speeds up the way the brain and body work. It makes the heart and lungs work faster. Cocaine also produces a strong sense of pleasure. Users say that it makes them feel more energetic. This feeling of pleasure is called euphoria.

The effects of cocaine may last from 5 to 40 minutes. But when the effects wear off, users often feel terrible. They may feel nervous, irritable, confused, angry, and tired. This feeling is called a cocaine crash. *(See: crash.)* One reason cocaine users want to take more of the drug is to avoid crashing.

Cocaine can hurt the body. Cocaine users may suffer from headaches, sore throats, vomiting, sleeplessness, nosebleeds, muscle pains, coughing, and sinus problems. Using cocaine can disrupt the regular pumping of the heart, leading to a sudden heart attack. It can cause permanent damage to the brain and lungs. Cocaine use by pregnant women can also cause severe damage to unborn children.

Cocaine is a psychoactive drug: it changes the thoughts and feelings of the people who use it. *(See: psychoactive drug.)* Cocaine users may become easily upset and highly suspicious of other people. They may get very depressed and think about committing suicide. They may find it difficult to think clearly; they may lose interest in everyday activities. *(See: amotivational syndrome.)* Cocaine users may also suffer from hallucinations. *(See: hallucination.)* One common hallucination is the feeling that insects, called coke bugs, are crawling beneath the skin.

Cocaine is a highly addictive drug. *(See: addiction.)* Some scientists believe that it is easier to become addicted to cocaine than to any other drug. Repeated cocaine use quickly leads to tolerance, or the need for more of a drug to get the same effect. *(See: tolerance.)* Users can also develop dependence on cocaine, which means that they need to use cocaine to feel normal and to avoid the pain of withdrawal. *(See: dependence, withdrawal.)* For these reasons, it can be very hard for people to stop using cocaine once they start.❐

Cocaine: Facts and Figures

- Over 21 million people in the United States have used cocaine.

- The number of cocaine users is decreasing. In 1985, 12.2 million people used cocaine or crack; in 1990, 8.2 million people used the drug.

- The number of people using cocaine regularly is increasing, from 647,000 in 1985 to 862,000 in 1990.

- 11% of regular cocaine users use the drug once a week; 4% use the drug daily or almost daily.

- 5% of eighth-grade students and 9% of tenth-grade students have tried cocaine.

- The number of hospital emergencies involving the use of cocaine or crack increased from 8,831 in 1984 to 46,020 in 1988. The number of cocaine-related deaths rose from 628 in 1984 to 1,589 in 1988.

- More young people are now aware of the dangers of using cocaine. In 1985, only 31% of young people thought that using cocaine was a "great risk"; the latest survey shows that 53% believe that cocaine use is very dangerous.

codeine:
   a drug made from the opium poppy. Drugs that are made from the juice of the opium poppy are called opiates. *(See: opiate.)* Although codeine is one of the opiate drugs, it is not nearly as strong or addictive as opium, morphine, or heroin. Codeine is often used as a medicine to treat pain, to control coughs, and to stop diarrhea. *(See: heroin, morphine, opium.)*

coke:
   a slang term for cocaine. *(See: cocaine.)*

coke bugs:
   See: cocaine, hallucination.

corticosteroids:
   a group of hormones made by the body's adrenal glands. Synthetic corticosteroids are often used as a medicine to help treat such conditions as skin rashes, allergies, and arthritis. They also help the body to adjust to stress and recover from physical injuries. Corticosteroid medicines include cortisone and prednisone.
   Corticosteroids are often confused with anabolic steroids. Anabolic steroids are a synthetic form of the body's natural male hormone, testosterone. They are rarely used as medicine. Anabolic steroids promote the growth of muscle tissue, and

they are commonly used by athletes and body builders as a short cut to a more muscular body. *(See: anabolic steroids.)*

crack:

a hard, rocklike form of cocaine; also called rock. *(See: cocaine.)* Crack is a form of cocaine that is made to be smoked. It gets its name from the crackling sound it makes as it burns.

Crack is a very addictive form of cocaine. *(See: addiction.)* Because it is smoked, the effects of the drug are felt within seconds, and they are very strong. The effects of crack last from 5 to 20 minutes. When the effects wear off, crack users crash and usually feel very sick. *(See: crash.)* For this reason, they want to take the drug again and again. The result can be cocaine addiction. Both medical experts and drug addicts agree that the repeated use of crack is the quickest way to get addicted to cocaine.

crack house:

a house where crack is made and sold. *(See: crack.)*

crash:

a sick feeling that drug users get when the effects of a drug, especially a stimulant drug, wear off. *(See: stimulant.)* A crash makes drug users depressed and irritable. Drug users often want to use more drugs to avoid or to stop crashing.

dealer:

a person who sells illegal drugs; also called a pusher.

denial:

when a person refuses to believe that he or she has a drug problem. Many people who are addicted to drugs deny that they have a drug problem. They may think that they can stop using drugs whenever they want. They may say that everyone else is using drugs or that they are not really hurting anyone.

There are many different ways to deny a drug problem. But denying a drug problem doesn't make it go away. It only makes matters worse because it keeps addicts from getting the treatment and counseling they need. The first step toward recovery from drug addiction is for an addict to admit that he or she has a drug problem. *(See: enabling.)*

dependence:

when the body and brain need a drug to avoid feeling sick. Dependence means that drug use has changed the brain and body so much that people need drugs to feel normal. A person who is dependent on drugs needs them to avoid the painful symptoms of withdrawal. *(See: addiction, withdrawal.)*

depressant:

a kind of drug that slows down, or depresses, the way the brain and body work. Alcohol is one kind of depressant. *(See: alcohol.)* Other depressant drugs, also called downers, are barbiturates, sedatives, and tranquilizers.

Depressant drugs first slow down the cerebral cortex, the part of the brain that controls our senses, movements, and thoughts. Even a small amount of a depressant can slow down the activity of the cerebral cortex, giving the user a calm and relaxed feeling. *(See: psychoactive drug.)*

Depressants can disrupt the messages to and from the brain that control our senses, making it difficult to see and hear clearly. They can disrupt the messages that control our movements, making it difficult to walk straight and even to stand up. They can also disrupt the messages that control our thoughts, making it difficult to think clearly, to pay attention, and to remember things. Too strong a dose of a depressant drug, called an overdose, can even turn off the brain entirely. An overdose can shut down the part of the brain that controls the heartbeat and breathing, causing death. *(See: overdose.)*

Barbiturates, sedatives, and tranquilizers are used by doctors as medicine. Doctors may prescribe them to try to change the mood or behavior of some patients. But these drugs can be dangerous if not used properly, and they may be bought and used only with a doctor's prescription. *(See: medicine.)*

designer drugs:

a term for illegal synthetic drugs. *(See: synthetic drug.)*

detoxification:

the process of getting drugs out of the body. The word "toxin" means poison, and detoxification means cleaning the poison of drugs out of the body. It is an early and important step in recovery from addiction. *(See: addiction, recovery.)*

dope:

a slang term for illegal drugs.

dose:

the amount of a medicine or drug taken at one time.

downer:

a slang term for a depressant drug. *(See: depressant.)*

drinking problem:

when a person drinks alcohol too much and too often. A drinking problem gets people in trouble. It may disrupt family life or make it hard for someone at school or work. A drinking problem often gets people in trouble with the police. Although it is against the law for people under the age of 21 to use alcohol, surveys show that one out of every five teenagers has a drinking problem. And drinking problems can easily lead to alcohol addiction. *(See: addiction, alcohol.)*

The Warning Signs of a Drinking Problem

Someone with a drinking problem needs help. So it is important that people know the warning signs of a drinking problem. Here are some of them:

- missing a lot of school or work
- a sudden change in performance at school or work
- withdrawing from friends or relatives, or a lack of interest in everyday activities
- strange and unexpected mood changes
- "hanging out" with people who drink
- drinking alone or drinking at odd times
- talking or thinking about alcohol a lot
- drinking just to get drunk
- drinking to cope with stressful situations or to deal with problems
- lying about drinking or stealing money to buy alcohol
- hiding alcohol or sneaking drinks
- reckless behavior while drinking

drug:

a substance that changes how the body and brain work. Drugs that change the way people think, feel, and behave are called psychoactive drugs. *(See: psychoactive drug.)* Some kinds of psychoactive drugs, like caffeine, are legal for everyone to use, though they can still be harmful if not used properly. Some drugs, like alcohol, are so strong that they are legal only for adults to use. And some drugs, like cocaine and marijuana, are so dangerous that they are illegal for everyone to use.

Many medicines are also psychoactive drugs. Like other drugs, medicines can also be dangerous to use. They should be used with care and with adult supervision. *(See: medicine.)*

drunk:

a slang term for intoxicated. *(See: alcohol.)*

DWI:

the abbreviation for "driving while intoxicated." Drunk driving is also referred to as "driving under the influence" of alcohol. *(See: alcohol.)* It is illegal for people to drive if they have had too much alcohol to drink. Each state has strict laws about drinking and driving. Most states use some measure of blood alcohol content (BAC) to decide when someone has had too much to drink. *(See: BAC.)* But in every state, it is against the law for anyone under the age of 21 to use alcohol.

Drinking and Driving: Facts and Figures

- Drunk driving is the most frequently committed crime in the United States today. Each year, almost 2 million people are arrested for drunk driving.

- 50% of all traffic deaths are related to alcohol.

- Each year, drunk driving crashes kill nearly 24,000 people—an average of one death every 22 minutes. In the last 10 years, as many as 250,000 people were killed in drunk driving crashes.

- Each year, over 650,000 people are injured in drunk driving crashes—an average of one every minute.

- Drinking and driving is the number-one killer of teenagers. Over 3,500 teenagers are killed each year in car crashes involving alcohol. Over 10 teenagers die each day in drunk driving crashes.

- 40% of all people will be involved in an alcohol-related car crash at some time in their lives.

- The annual cost in property damage and medical costs due to drunk driving is more than $24 billion.

enabling:

when people allow or make it possible for someone they know to continue using drugs. The family and friends of a drug user, often without even knowing it, may do things that encourage further drug use. They may refuse to believe that there is a drug problem. Or they may "look the other way" when they see evidence of a drug problem. They may try to "rescue" a person who uses drugs from the many problems caused by drug addiction. They may make excuses for drug users, or lend them money, or take over their responsibilities. This kind of enabling only makes it easier for a person with a drug problem to continue using drugs. *(See: denial.)*

endorphin:

a kind of chemical produced within the body that acts on the brain like the opiate drugs. The term endorphin comes from "endogenous morphine," which means "the morphine within the body." *(See: opiate.)*

euphoria:

a feeling of great happiness and pleasure; a term used to describe one of the effects of drugs like cocaine and heroin.

F

fix:

a slang term for a dose of heroin. *(See: heroin.)*

flashback:

when people who have used the hallucinogen LSD get the effects of the drug after they have stopped using it. *(See: LSD.)* A flashback may occur, suddenly and without warning, even though the drug has not been used for a long time.

G

gateway drug:

a drug that may lead to the use of other drugs. Alcohol, nicotine, and marijuana are called gateway drugs because they seem to "open the gate" to drug problems. Many people with drug problems report that these are the drugs that they first used. But it should also be remembered that alcohol, nicotine, and marijuana are dangerous drugs, too, even if they do not lead to the use of other drugs.

germ:

a slang term for a tiny microorganism that causes infectious diseases. The term is used for both bacteria and viruses. *(See: bacteria, immune system, virus.)*

grass:

a slang term for marijuana. *(See: marijuana.)*

hallucination:

a distorted sensory impression. Hallucinations are sights and sounds that are not real. Psychoactive drugs, especially hallucinogens, disrupt the way the brain controls the senses, causing the appearance of everyday objects to seem strange and unusual. *(See: hallucinogen, psychoactive drug.)*

The term "hallucinate" means "to dream." Dreams are a normal and natural activity of the brain. Hallucinations, like dreams, can be strange, confusing, and sometimes frightening. Unlike dreams, however, hallucinations are not a normal or natural activity of the brain. They are a sign that something is wrong with the brain.

hallucinogen:

a kind of psychoactive drug that changes the way the world looks. Hallucinogens change the way people who use them see and hear the world. They change everyday sights and sounds in strange, confusing, and sometimes frightening ways. These changes in the way the world appears are called hallucinations. *(See: hallucination, psychoactive drug.)*

There are several kinds of hallucinogenic drugs. Some are natural drugs, which means they come from plant sources. The most widely used natural hallucinogens come from the peyote cactus and several kinds of mushrooms. *(See: "magic" mushroom, peyote.)* Other hallucinogenic drugs are synthetic, which means they are made in a laboratory. The two most widely used synthetic hallucinogens are LSD and PCP. *(See: LSD, PCP.)* Marijuana is often considered an hallucinogenic drug, too. *(See: marijuana.)* A new group of illegal synthetic drugs called designer drugs also includes some hallucinogens.

Hallucinogens change the way the brain normally works. They upset the balance of chemicals in the brain and disrupt the way the brain controls senses, thoughts, and emotions. Our senses give us clear and accurate information about the world around us, but hallucinogenic drugs cause people to see and hear things in unusual and distorted ways. The shape, color, and appearance of objects may change again and again. Other objects may seem to melt, to disappear, or to float away.

Our thoughts enable us to know and understand the world around us, but hallucinogenic drugs make it hard to think clearly or to make good decisions. Our emotions allow us to react to the world around us, but hallucinogenic drugs often cause people to lose control of their feelings, making them sad or happy, angry or afraid, for no reason.

There are serious long-term effects from the repeated use of hallucinogenic drugs, too. People who use hallucinogens regularly develop tolerance to them, which means they need bigger, and more dangerous, doses of these drugs to get the same effect. *(See: tolerance.)* The long-term use of hallucinogens may also lead to mood or personality changes, making people nervous, or depressed, or easily upset. It may lead to a loss of interest in everyday activities. *(See: amotivational syndrome.)*

hangover:

a sick feeling that people get after the effects of a drug wear off. The term is mostly used to describe the feelings that follow the heavy use of alcohol. The typical hangover includes headaches, muscle aches, nausea or upset stomach, and feelings of fatigue and depression. *(See: alcohol.)*

hemp:

another word for the cannabis or marijuana plant.
(See: cannabis, marijuana.)

heroin:

a drug made from the opium poppy. Drugs that are made from the juice of the opium poppy are called opiates. *(See: opiate.)* When heroin was developed in the late 1800s, scientists hoped it would be a safe and effective medicine. But it was soon clear that heroin is a highly addictive drug.

Heroin is the strongest and most addictive of the opiates. *(See: addiction.)* It is twice as strong as morphine and 20 times as strong as crude opium. *(See: morphine, opium.)* Heroin use quickly leads to tolerance, which means that users need more and more of the drug to get the same effect, and dependence, which means that users need the drug to avoid withdrawal symptoms. *(See: dependence, tolerance, withdrawal.)*

Heroin is a white powder that is commonly dissolved in water and injected into the body with a hypodermic needle. *(See: hypodermic syringe.)* Heroin is a psychoactive drug: using it changes the way the brain works. Like other opiates, heroin produces a strong feeling of pleasure, or euphoria. But also like other opiate drugs, heroin depresses, or slows down, the messages that travel to and from the brain. *(See: depressant, psychoactive drug.)* Too strong a dose of heroin, called an overdose, can even shut down the messages that direct the lungs to breathe. *(See: overdose.)* And if heroin addicts share used or dirty needles, they also risk getting infectious diseases, like hepatitis, tetanus, and AIDS.

Heroin: Facts and Figures

- In 1990, there were between 500,000 and 750,000 heroin addicts in the United States.

- Over 200,000 heroin addicts live in the New York City area.

- The heroin brought into the United States comes from three major sources: Southeast Asia (Thailand Burma, and Laos), Southwest Asia (Pakistan, Iran, and Afghanistan), and Mexico.

- Law enforcement officials catch less than 10% of the heroin supply intended for the United States.

- 67% of heroin users are 30 years old or older; 10% of heroin users are between the ages of 12 and 17.

- One out of every 4 heroin addicts is female.

- 40% of heroin addicts are white; 40% are black.

- One out of every 3 people sent to prison has used heroin.

- Heroin was invented in 1874 and was a common medicine for many years. Heroin use was finally restricted by the Harrison Narcotic Act of 1914.

high:

a slang term for the pleasurable effects of a psychoactive drug. *(See: psychoactive drug.)* When people feel the effects of such a drug, they are said to "get high."❐

hooked:

a slang term for addicted. *(See: addiction.)*❐

hypodermic syringe:

a medical instrument used to inject fluids through the skin into the body. It is commonly referred to as a hypodermic needle. Although the hypodermic syringe is a very valuable medical device, it is also used by drug users to inject such dangerous substances as cocaine and heroin. By sharing used or dirty needles, drug users risk getting blood poisoning or such infectious diseases as hepatitis, tetanus, and AIDS.❐

ice:

a slang term for one kind of amphetamine that is made to be smoked. *(See: amphetamine, stimulant.)*❐

immune system:

the human body's natural system of self-defense against diseases caused by bacteria and viruses. *(See: bacteria, virus.)* This system of defense includes two important kinds of white blood cells: 1) lymphocytes, which produce antibodies that identify and mark invading germs, and 2) phagocytes, which surround germs and destroy them. The antibodies produced by the lymphocytes to fight a specific disease also give the body immunity, or the ability to resist infection, against that disease. If the body is again attacked by the same bacteria or virus, the lymphocytes quickly produce the antibodies that are needed to give the body protection against that disease. A group of medicines called vaccines is also used to help the body develop immunity against infectious diseases. Vaccines contain a dead or a weakened form of disease-causing germs. Although vaccines are too weak to cause the disease that the germs usually produce, the lymphocytes make the antibodies needed to give the body protection against a future infection.

immunity:

the ability to resist infection and disease. *(See: immune system.)*

intoxicated:

when alcohol builds up in the body. *(See: alcohol.)*

J

joint:
a slang term for a cigarette made from marijuana. *(See: marijuana.)*

junk:
a slang term for heroin. *(See: heroin.)*

junkie:
a slang term for a person addicted to heroin. *(See: addiction, heroin.)*

L

legal drinking age:
the age at which people may legally buy and use alcohol. In the United States, the legal drinking age is decided by the individual states. Although the laws about drinking vary from state to state, the legal drinking age in each of the states is now 21 years old. *(See: alcohol.)*

LSD:
the abbreviation for lysergic acid diethylamide. LSD is one of several kinds of drugs, called hallucinogens, that cause people to see and hear the world in strange and distorted ways. *(See: hallucinogen.)* These sensory distortions are called hallucinations. *(See: hallucination.)*

LSD, or acid, is a synthetic hallucinogen, which means it is made in a laboratory. It is a tasteless, colorless, odorless drug. In the laboratory, pure LSD is a white powder. When it is sold, LSD often takes the form of tablets or capsules. As a liquid, LSD can be swallowed by adding it to sugar cubes, thin squares of gelatin called window panes, or an absorbent tissue called blotter paper.

LSD is one of the strongest psychoactive drugs ever made. *(See: psychoactive drug.)* It is 100 times stronger than psilocybin and over 4,000 times stronger than mescaline. *(See: mescaline, psilocybin.)* Like other hallucinogens, LSD disrupts the way the brain controls the senses, thoughts, and emotions. In addition to distorting sensory images, LSD makes it difficult to think clearly, to pay attention, and to make good judgments. People who use LSD may suffer from sudden mood changes. They may become confused or scared of the world around them. They may feel alone, helpless, and completely out of control. In some cases, these effects have been known to recur, without warning, long after LSD use has stopped. *(See: flashback.)*

"magic" mushroom:

a kind of mushroom that is the source of hallucinogenic drugs. *(See: hallucinogen.)* Only a very few of the 6,000 different kinds of mushrooms contain hallucinogens. One of the more common of these so-called "magic" mushrooms contains the natural hallucinogenic drug psilocybin. *(See: psilocybin.)*

Like other hallucinogenic drugs, psilocybin changes the way the brain controls the senses, thoughts, and emotions. Psilocybin disrupts the way people see and hear the world (causing strange sensory distortions, or hallucinations); makes it difficult for people to think clearly, to pay attention, and to make good decisions; and causes sudden changes in moods and emotions. *(See: hallucination, psychoactive drug.)*❑

marijuana:

a drug that comes from the cannabis, or hemp, plant. *(See: cannabis.)* Marijuana, also called grass or pot, is made from the dried leaves and flowering tops of the cannabis plant. The cannabis plant contains over 400 chemicals, but the effects of marijuana are due to one chemical: tetrahydrocannabinol, or THC, the primary psychoactive ingredient in marijuana. *(See: psychoactive drug.)* Marijuana is most often smoked in handmade cigarettes called joints, though some people cook with it or brew it in a marijuana tea.

Many scientists classify marijuana as an hallucinogenic drug. *(See: hallucinogen.)* Like other hallucinogens, marijuana disrupts the way the brain controls the senses. It can cause sensory distortions, or hallucinations, but only if very strong doses of the drug are used. *(See: hallucination.)* Marijuana also disrupts the way the brain controls thoughts and emotions. It makes it difficult to think clearly, to pay attention, to perform ordinary tasks, and to remember things. Marijuana use can change people's moods, making them nervous, easily upset, and suspicious of other people. It can cause a panic reaction, which is a feeling that things are completely out of control.

Repeated marijuana use leads to tolerance, which means that people need more of the drug to get the same effect. The regular use of marijuana can also lead to dependence, meaning that people need the drug to feel normal. *(See: dependence, tolerance.)* Long-term marijuana use can cause people to lose all interest in everyday activities. *(See: amotivational syndrome.)*

Marijuana can also harm the body. The long-term use of marijuana damages the cells of the brain and nervous system. Smoking marijuana causes lung cancer and may lead to heart disease. Marijuana also destroys the body's white blood cells. These cells help fight infections, so it is likely that marijuana users will get sick more often than other people.

Marijuana: Facts and Figures

- Today, marijuana is the most widely used illegal drug. Over 65 million people in the United States have used marijuana. Over 25 million people used marijuana in the last year. Over 11 million people use it at least once a month. Over 6 million people use marijuana every day.

- One out of every 7 people in drug abuse treatment programs reports problems with marijuana.

- Smoking a single marijuana cigarette is as harmful as smoking 5 cigarettes made of tobacco.

- Marijuana smoke contains more than 400 different chemicals. Some of these chemicals can stay in the body for months.

- Fewer young people are using marijuana than in the past. In 1985, 5.8% of 12 and 13 year olds used marijuana; in 1988, that number was down to 4.2%.

- More young people know that smoking marijuana is very dangerous. In 1987, 37% of young people thought that smoking marijuana was a "great risk"; in 1988, that number increased to 44%.

medicine:

a large group of drugs used to help fight sickness and disease. Medicines do many different things. Some medicines are drugs that fight infectious diseases. *(See: immune system.)* Some are drugs that help to ease pain. *(See: analgesic, anesthetic, opiate.)* And some medicines are drugs that act on the brain to change people's emotions and behavior. *(See: psychoactive drug.)* Although medicines are an important part of the fight against sickness and disease, it should be remembered that they are drugs and can be dangerous if not used properly.◻

mescaline:

a natural hallucinogenic drug that is the active ingredient in the peyote cactus. *(See: hallucinogen, peyote.)*◻

morphine:

a drug made from the opium poppy. Drugs that are made from the juice of the opium poppy are called opiates. *(See: opiate.)* Morphine is made from crude opium. *(See: opium.)* The white morphine crystals can be crushed and made into pills or capsules. More often, morphine crystals are dissolved in water and injected into the bloodstream with a hypodermic needle. *(See: hypodermic syringe.)*

Morphine is a strong opiate. It is 10 times stronger than opium. Its strength makes morphine valuable as a medicine.

Doctors may give morphine to patients who are suffering from serious pain. But morphine is also a highly addictive drug. Though it is safe and effective as a medicine, morphine can be dangerous if not used properly. *(See: addiction, medicine.)*

narcotic:

another word for an opiate drug. *(See: opiate.)*

natural drug:

a kind of drug that comes from or is made from plant, animal, or mineral sources.

Some Natural Drugs and Their Sources	
Opiates	the opium poppy
Cocaine	the coca plant
Marijuana	the cannabis (hemp) plant
Nicotine	the tobacco plant
Mescaline	the peyote cactus
Psilocybin	"magic" mushrooms
Caffeine	coffee beans, tea leaves, cocoa beans, cola nuts

nicotine:
a drug that comes from the leaves of the tobacco plant. Nicotine is a colorless, oily liquid found in products made from tobacco, including cigarettes, cigars, pipe tobacco, chewing tobacco, and a powdery form of tobacco called snuff.

Most people who use tobacco products smoke cigarettes. When tobacco products like cigarettes are burned, they release poisonous gases that can seriously damage the lungs and the heart. Tobacco smoke also contains thousands of chemicals that form a thick, gummy paste known as tar. Tar is a leading cause of lung diseases, like emphysema and bronchitis, and many types of cancer, a disease that attacks and destroys the body's healthy cells and tissues. Other tobacco products are also dangerous to use. They can cause diseases of the mouth, throat, and stomach.

Nicotine is a highly addictive substance, which is why it is so hard for people to stop using tobacco products once they start. Tobacco use quickly leads to tolerance, causing users to need more nicotine to get the same effect they used to get, and to dependence, causing users to need nicotine to avoid withdrawal. *(See: addiction, dependence, tolerance, withdrawal.)*

The use of tobacco by pregnant women can severely hurt their unborn children. And breathing in other people's smoke, called secondhand or passive smoking, causes serious health problems, too. *(See: secondhand smoking.)*

Nicotine: Facts and Figures

- Smokers are 10 times as likely as nonsmokers to develop lung cancer. Smokers are 3 times as likely to die from a heart attack at an early age.

- Smoking tobacco products is the leading cause of early death among adults (390,000 deaths per year).

- 130,000 people die each year from cancer due to smoking cigarettes; 170,000 people die each year from heart disease due to smoking cigarettes.

- 70% of all young people try cigarettes; 40% of them try cigarettes before they enter high school.

- 18% of high-school seniors are daily smokers.

- 12% of boys have tried chewing tobacco or snuff.

- One out of every 4 teenage girls is a smoker.

- Nicotine is a very addictive drug. Fewer than 20% of smokers are able to quit the first time they try.

- Cigarette smoke contains 4,000 harmful chemicals.

- The number of people who smoke is going down. In 1965, 40% of adults smoked. Today, only 29% of adults smoke.

opiate:

a kind of drug that comes from the opium poppy. The scientific name for the opium poppy is *Papaver somniferum*. It means "the poppy that brings sleep." The opium poppy got its name because opiate drugs make people sleepy. Opiates belong to a group of drugs known as narcotics. The term "narcotic" means "to make numb" or "to take away feeling." The term refers to the fact that narcotics are able to ease pain.

Opiates are made from the juice of the opium poppy. The milky white juice of the poppy seedpods is dried to form a gummy, dark brown paste called crude opium. Crude opium is used to make the opiate drugs. These drugs include opium, codeine, morphine, and heroin. *(See: codeine, heroin, morphine, opium.)* Some opiates can be eaten or taken in liquid form; other opiates can be smoked or injected into the body with a hypodermic needle. *(See: hypodermic syringe.)*

Opiates are psychoactive drugs, which means that they change the way the brain normally works. *(See: psychoactive drug.)* They change the brain so that an opiate user does not feel pain. Because opiates change the brain in this way, they can be very useful as medicine. Opiates have been used for thousands of years to ease pain, to control diarrhea, and to calm people down when they are nervous, depressed, or not able to sleep. When they are used under the guidance of a doctor, opiate medicines can be safe and effective.

But opiates can also change the brain to produce a feeling of great pleasure, or euphoria, and some people use opiates simply because they like the pleasurable effects of these drugs. However, when opiates are not used as medicine, they can be quite dangerous. Opiates are highly addictive. *(See: addiction.)* Opiate use can quickly lead to tolerance, which causes users to need more of these drugs to get the same effect they used to get, and dependence, causing users to need these drugs to avoid the painful symptoms of withdrawal. *(See: dependence, tolerance, withdrawal.)*

opium:

a drug made from the opium poppy. Drugs that are made from the juice of the opium poppy are called opiates. *(See: opiate.)* For thousands of years, opium products were used as medicines. They were used to ease pain and to treat diarrhea. They were also used to make people calm and to help them sleep. But opium was not a reliable medicine, and like other opiate drugs, it was addictive. *(See: addiction.)* So doctors and scientists searched for new opiate medicines, a search that led to the discovery of the other opiate drugs—morphine, codeine, and heroin. *(See: codeine, heroin, morphine.)*

OTC drug:

the abbreviation for "over-the-counter" drug, the kind of drug that can be purchased without a doctor's prescription.❒

overdose:

too strong a dose of a drug, leading to illness, injury, or even death.❒

panic reaction:

a feeling that everything is out of control. Panic reactions can be brought on by such psychoactive drugs as marijuana, cocaine, and hallucinogens. *(See: psychoactive drug.)*❒

passive smoking:

(See: secondhand smoking.)❒

PCP:

the abbreviation for phencyclidine. PCP is one of a group of drugs, called hallucinogens, that cause the people who use them to see and hear the world in distorted and sometimes frightening ways. *(See: hallucinogen, psychoactive drug.)*

Although pure PCP is a white powder, it is sold and used in several forms. PCP can be swallowed, sniffed or snorted through the nose, or injected into the body with a hypodermic needle. *(See: hypodermic syringe.)* PCP powder is also sprinkled on marijuana cigarettes, or joints, and smoked.

PCP, also called angel dust, is by far the most dangerous of the hallucinogenic drugs. Using PCP can lead to heart and lung failure. Like other hallucinogens, PCP interferes with the way the brain controls the senses, movements, thoughts, and emotions. PCP use makes it hard for people to see and hear clearly. It can cause sensory distortions, or hallucinations. *(See: hallucination.)* PCP disrupts muscular control and can cause convulsions, a violent shaking of the muscles. However, PCP's most dangerous effect is what it does to the mind. Users may become nervous, confused, overly suspicious of other people, and very violent. PCP can also hurt unborn children if women use the drug when they are pregnant.

PCP users quickly develop tolerance to the drug and need more and more of it. They also become dependent on PCP to feel normal; if PCP users stop taking the drug, they may go through withdrawal. *(See: dependence, tolerance, withdrawal.)*

Using PCP is against the law. But PCP is the most widely used hallucinogen today. About one in 20 high-school seniors use PCP each year. Half of them started using PCP before they entered the tenth grade.❐

peer pressure:
the feeling that you have to do something because other people are doing it. It means doing something because you want to "fit in" or be "one of the crowd." Peer pressure is one of the reasons young people most often give for starting to use drugs.❑

pep pill:
a slang term for stimulants. *(See: stimulant.)*❑

peyote:
the source of mescaline. Mescaline is one of a group of drugs, called hallucinogens, that cause people to see and hear the world in distorted ways. *(See: hallucinogen, mescaline.)*

Peyote is a kind of cactus plant. The top of the cactus holds a little crown or button. This peyote button contains a natural hallucinogenic drug called mescaline. Mescaline is the active hallucinogenic ingredient in the peyote cactus.

Like other hallucinogenic drugs, mescaline changes the way the brain works. *(See: psychoactive drug.)* It disrupts the way the brain controls the senses, causing sensory distortions, or hallucinations. *(See: hallucination.)* Mescaline also disrupts the way the brain controls thinking, which makes it difficult for people to think clearly and to use good judgment, and the emotions, which causes sudden mood changes.❑

pot:
a slang term for marijuana. *(See: marijuana.)*

prescription drug:
a kind of drug that can be purchased and used only with a doctor's written order.

psilocybin:
a natural hallucinogen that is the psychoactive ingredient in one kind of "magic" mushroom. *(See: hallucinogen, "magic" mushroom, psychoactive drug.)*

psychoactive drug:
a kind of drug that changes the way the brain works. The word "psyche" means "mind"; the word "active" means "to act." Psychoactive drugs act on the brain to change the way people think, feel, and behave. These drugs include alcohol and other depressants, opiates, cocaine and other stimulants, marijuana, hallucinogens, and some medicines.

Messages to and from the different parts of the brain and central nervous system control everything we do. They control our senses, movements, thoughts, and emotions. These messages travel along a network of nerve cells called neurons. Between each neuron, there is a gap called a synapse. It takes a special chemical called a transmitter to get a message across the synapses between nerve cells. There are many different kinds of transmitters in the brain, and they help send different kinds of messages. Some carry the messages that control our muscles. Some help send messages of pain and pleasure. Some control our thoughts and emotions.

Psychoactive drugs upset the balance of these chemical transmitters, changing the way messages travel to and from the different parts of the brain. They may disrupt the way the senses normally work, causing strange and distorted images. They may disrupt the way the muscles work, making it hard to control body movements. They may disrupt the way our thoughts and emotions work, making it hard to think clearly and causing mood changes.

Doctors prescribe psychoactive drugs as medicine for a variety of reasons. Some psychoactive drugs help to control pain. Others help to change the mood or behavior of a patient. If used under proper medical guidance, some psychoactive drugs can help people lead better lives. But drugs that change the way the brain normally works can be dangerous, too. They can damage the body and brain. They can lead to dependence and addiction. *(See: addiction, dependence, medicine.)* Even very helpful medicines can be harmful if not used properly.❐

pusher:

a person who sells illegal drugs; also called a dealer.❐

R

recovery:

the process by which drug users recover from the sickness of addiction. *(See: addiction.)* The first step toward recovery is for an addict to admit that he or she has a drug problem and to seek professional treatment. *(See: denial.)* With the help of doctors and drug abuse counselors, addicts can then detoxify, or clean out the poison of drugs from the body and brain, and begin to learn new, drug-free habits. Recovery is the process by which drug addicts learn what made them use drugs in the past and how to say "No" to drugs in the future. It is a difficult process, but addicts can learn to live drug-free lives.

reefer:

a slang term for marijuana or a marijuana cigarette. *(See: joint, marijuana.)*

rock:

a slang term for crack cocaine. *(See: crack.)*

"roid" rage:

violent behavior caused by the use of anabolic steroids. *(See: anabolic steroids.)*

secondhand smoking:

breathing in other people's smoke. Secondhand smoking, also called passive smoking, is very unhealthy. It causes lung and heart diseases and can lead to cancer. People who live in homes or work in offices with smokers tend to be sick more often than people who live and work in smoke-free areas.

sedative:

one of several kinds of drugs known as depressants. *(See: depressant.)*

smuggle:

to bring drugs into a country illegally. A person who tries to bring drugs into a country illegally is called a smuggler.

sober:

when the body is free of alcohol. *(See: alcohol.)*

speed:

a slang term for amphetamines. *(See: amphetamine.)*

steroids:

See: anabolic steroids.

stimulant:

a kind of drug that stimulates, or speeds up, the way the brain and body work. Cocaine is one kind of stimulant. So are amphetamines, also called speed, uppers, and pep pills. Amphetamines are often taken as pills, but they can also be snorted through the nose, smoked, or injected into the body with a hypodermic needle. *(See: cocaine, hypodermic syringe.)*

Users report that stimulants make them more alert and energetic. But the use of stimulant drugs is very dangerous. It can cause serious damage to the body, including stomach ulcers, skin disorders, weight loss, brain damage, and diseases of the lungs, liver, kidneys, and heart. Stimulants can disrupt the messages from the brain that control the heart and the lungs. Too strong a dose, called an overdose, can cause death from a sudden heart attack, stroke (bursting of blood vessels), or failure of the lungs to keep breathing. *(See: overdose.)*

Like other psychoactive drugs, stimulants also change the way the brain works. They change the moods and emotions of the people who use them. The repeated use of stimulants leads to nervousness, anxiety, sleeplessness, and depression. People who use amphetamines regularly also become easily upset and very suspicious of other people. And the long-term use of stimulant drugs may lead to psychosis, or severe mental illness. *(See: psychoactive drug.)*

Caffeine is also a mild stimulant. *(See: caffeine.)*

synthetic drug:

a kind of drug that is made in a laboratory.
(See: natural drug.)

testosterone:

the natural male hormone. (See: anabolic steroids.)

THC:

the abbreviation for the chemical tetrahydrocannabinol, the primary psychoactive ingredient in marijuana.
(See: marijuana, psychoactive drug.)

tolerance:

the way the brain and body need more and more of a drug to get the same effect. Tolerance means that the amount of a drug that used to change the way the brain works is no longer enough to do so. Because the nerve cells of the brain have gotten used to the drug, the drug no longer affects the work of the brain as much at it used to. This is why drug addicts must continually take bigger, and more dangerous, doses of the drugs they use. (See: addiction, psychoactive drug.)

tranquilizer:
one of several kinds of drugs known as depressants. *(See: depressant.)*

upper:
a slang term for amphetamines. *(See: amphetamine.)*

vaccine:
a dead or weakened dose of a disease-causing bacterium or virus. Vaccines help protect the body against a variety of infectious diseases. *(See: bacteria, immune system, virus.)*

virus:
tiny microorganisms that can cause diseases if they infect the body. Different viruses cause different sicknesses, such as the common cold, measles, and AIDS.

window pane:

a thin square of gelatin that is used to hold a dose of the hallucinogenic drug LSD. *(See: hallucinogen, LSD.)*

wine:

an alcoholic beverage made from grapes or other fruits and plants. *(See: alcohol.)*

withdrawal:

the sick and painful feelings that people get when they stop using the drugs they are dependent on. *(See: dependence.)* The symptoms of drug withdrawal can be quite serious and may include cramps, chills, sleeplessness, nausea and severe vomiting, headaches, and sensitivity to light and noise. Mood and personality changes are also common. Drug users going through withdrawal may be irritable, nervous, tense, and very easily upset. They may be depressed, tired, and "worn out." But most of all, they feel a strong craving for more drugs. The desire to avoid withdrawal symptoms often leads drug users to take drugs again and again.

How to Use
The Drug-Alert Resource Guide

The Drug-Alert Resource Guide is designed to give you a survey of drug-related programs and activities. The organizations listed here can provide information and assistance.

The Resource Guide is divided into six categories:

- **Hotlines:** drug counseling and referral services

- **Private Agencies:** drug prevention, education, and counseling programs. Other national organizations (not specifically drug related and therefore not listed here) are also working to prevent the use of drugs. Check your local phone directory.

- **U.S. State Agencies:** for each state, four resources are given (when available): state legislature, governor's office, health office, and education office.

- **U.S. Federal Agencies:** by cabinet office or cabinet-level office

- **Regional Centers for Drug-Free Schools:** regional drug education and training centers

- **Canadian Resources**

HOTLINES

These hotlines offer counseling
and referral services to individuals and families.
They operate 24 hours a day, 7 days a week.

National Child Safety
   Council Hotline
P.O. Box 1368
Jackson, MI 49204
800/222-1464

National Council on Alcoholism
   and Drug Dependency Hotline
12 W. 21st St.
New York, NY 10010
800/622-2255

National Cocaine Hotline
P.O. Box 100
Summit, NJ 07901
800/262-2463

Open Quest Institute Hotline
446 S. Marengo
Pasadena, CA 91101
800/333-4313

National Institute on Drug Abuse
(NIDA) Hotline
NIDA Information and Treatment Center
Social Scientific Systems, Inc.
12280 Wilkens Ave., 1st Floor
Rockville, MD 20852
800/662-4357

PRIVATE AGENCIES

Action on Smoking & Health
2013 H St., NW
Washington, D.C. 20006
202/659-4310
(nicotine/tobacco)

Al-Anon Family Group Headquarters
P.O. Box 862, Midtown Station
New York, NY 10018
212/302-7240
800/344-2666
(alcohol)

Alcoholics Anonymous
P.O. Box 459
Grand Central Station
New York, NY 10163
212/686-1100
(alcohol)

American Cancer Society
1599 Clifton Rd.
Atlanta, GA 30329
404/320-3333
800/227-2345
(nicotine/tobacco)

American Council on Alcoholism
The Health Education Center
White Marsh Business Center
5024 Campbell Blvd., Suite H
Baltimore, MD 21236
301/931-9393
(alcohol)

American Council for Drug Education
204 Monroe St., Suite 110
Rockville, MD 20850
301/294-0600

American Heart Association
7320 Greenville Ave.
Dallas, TX 75231
214/373-6300
800/527-6941
(nicotine/tobacco)

American Lung Association
1740 Broadway
New York, NY 10019
212/315-8700
(nicotine/tobacco)

Americans United for a Smoke-Free
  Society
8701 Georgia Ave., Suite 210
Silver Spring, MD 20910
202/667-6653
(nicotine/tobacco)

Cocaine Anonymous
3700 N.W. 7th Ave.
Pompano Beach, FL 33064
305/946-6357
(cocaine)

Committees of Correspondence
57 Conant St., Rm. 113
Danvers, MA 01923
508/774-2641

The Do It Now Foundation
P.O. Box 27568
Tempe, AZ 85285-7568
602/491-0393

Emphysema Anonymous
P.O. Box 3224
Seminole, FL 34642
813/391-9977
(nicotine/tobacco)

Families Anonymous
P.O. Box 528
Van Nuys, CA 91408
818/989-7841
800/736-9805

Families in Focus
The Cottage Program International
736 S. 500 East St.
Salt Lake City, UT 84102
800/752-6100
801/532-6185 in Salt Lake City

Just Say No International
1777 N. California Blvd., Rm. 200
Walnut Creek, CA 94596
800/258-2766
415/939-6666 in California

Mothers Against Drunk Driving (MADD)
Central Office
511 E. Carpenter Frwy., Suite 700
Irving, TX 75062
214/744-6233
(alcohol)

Nar-Anon Family Group Headquarters
P.O. Box 2562
Palos Verdes Peninsula, CA 90274
213/547-5800

Narcotics Anonymous
P.O. Box 9999
Van Nuys, CA 91409
818/780-3951

Narcotics Education
12501 Old Columbia Pike
Silver Spring, MD 20904-6600
301/680-6740
800/548-8700

National Association of Alcoholism
   & Drug Abuse Counselors
3717 Columbia Pike, Suite 300
Arlington, VA 22204
703/920-4644
800/548-0497

National Association for Children
   of Alcoholics
31582 Coast Hwy., Suite B
South Laguna, CA 92677
714/499-3889
(alcohol)

National Association of State Alcohol
   & Drug Abuse Directors
444 N. Capitol St. NW, Suite 642
Washington, D.C. 20001
202/783-6868

National Association on Drug Abuse
   Problems
355 Lexington Ave.
New York, NY 10017
212/986-1170

National Commission Against Drunk
   Driving
1140 Connecticut Ave. NW, Suite 804
Washington, D.C. 20036
202/452-0130
(alcohol)

National Congress of Parents
   & Teachers (PTA)
700 N. Rush St.
Chicago, IL 60611
312/787-0977

National Council on Alcoholism
12 W. 21st St.
New York, NY 10010
212/206-6770
800/NCA-CALL
(alcohol)

National Families in Action
2296 Henderson Mill Rd., Suite 204
Atlanta, GA 30345
404/934-6364

National Federation of Parents
   for Drug-Free Youth
Communications Center
1423 N. Jefferson St.
Springfield, MO 65802
417/836-3709

National Parents' Resource Institute
   for Drug Education (PRIDE)
The Hurt Bldg., Suite 210
50 Hurt Plaza
Atlanta, GA 30303
404/577-4500
800/677-7433

Parents Against Drug Abuse
95 White Bridge Rd.
P.O. Box 210529
Nashville, TN 37221-0529
615/320-8565

Parents' Association to Neutralize
   Drug & Alcohol Abuse
P.O. Box 314
Annandale, VA 22033
703/750-9285

Stop Teen-Age Addiction to Tobacco
   (STAT)
121 Lyman St., Suite 210
Springfield, MA 01103
413/732-7828
(nicotine/tobacco)

Students Against Driving Drunk (SADD)
P.O. Box 800
Marlboro, MA 01752
508/481-3568
(alcohol)

TARGET Resource Center
11724 Plaza Circle
P.O. Box 20626
Kansas City, MO 64195
800/366-6667

Toughlove
P.O. Box 1069
Doylestown, PA 18901
800/333-1069
215/348-7090

Youth to Youth
700 Bryden Rd.
Columbus, OH 43215
614/224-4506

STATE GOVERNMENT AGENCIES

Alabama

Legislative Reference Service
State House, Rm. 613
11 S. Union St.
Montgomery, AL 36130-6701
205/261-2500, ext. 7577

Governor's Office of Drug Abuse Policy
State House, Rm. 234
11 S. Union St.
Montgomery, AL 36130
205/261-7126

Div. of Mental Illness & Substance Abuse
Community Programs
Dept. of Mental Health
200 Interstate Park Dr.
P.O. Box 3710
Montgomery, AL 36193-5001
205/271-9253

Program Specialist
Drug Education Program
Dept. of Education
50 N. Ripley St.
Montgomery, AL 36130
205/242-8083

Alaska

Div. of Legal Services
Legislative Affairs Agency
Court Plaza Bldg., Rm. 500
P.O. Box Y
Juneau, AK 99811
907/465-3867

Special Assistant to the Governor
Anti-Drug Abuse Committee
P.O. Box A
Juneau, AK 99811
907/465-3500

Office of Alcoholism & Drug Abuse
Dept. of Health & Social Services
114 2nd St.
Pouch H-05F
Juneau, AK 99811
907/586-6201

Dept. of Education
Drug-Free Schools Program
P.O. Box F
Juneau, AK 99811-0500
907/465-2841

Arizona

Legislative Council
State Capitol
Legislative Services Wing, Rm. 100
1700 W. Washington St.
Phoenix, AZ 85007
602/255-4236

Director
Governor's Office of Substance Abuse
Alliance Against Drugs
State Capitol, Rm. 810
1700 W. Washington St.
Phoenix, AZ 85007
602/542-3456

Office of Community Behavioral Health
  Services
Dept. of Health Services
701 E. Jefferson St.
Phoenix, AZ 85304
602/255-1152

Chemical Abuse Prevention Specialist
Dept. of Education
1535 W. Jefferson St.
Phoenix, AZ 85007
602/255-3847

Arkansas

Bureau of Legislative Research
Legislative Council
State Capitol, Rm. 315
5th & Woodlane
Little Rock, AR 72201
501/371-1937

Arkansas Alcohol & Drug Abuse
  Coordinating Council
State Capitol, Suite 250
Little Rock, AR 72201
501/682-2345

Office on Alcohol & Drug Abuse
  Prevention
Dept. of Human Services
1515 W. 7th St., Suite 310
Little Rock, AR 72201
501/371-2604

Dept. of Education
Health, Physical Education,
  & Drug Education
#4 Capitol Mall, 405B
Little Rock, AR 72201-1071
501/682-4472

California

Assembly Office of Research
Committee on Policy Research Legislature
1100 J St., Rm. 535
Sacramento, CA 95814
916/445-1638

Chairman
Governor's Policy Council
111 Capitol Mall
Sacramento, CA 95814
916/445-1943

Dept. of Alcohol & Drug Programs
111 Capitol Mall
Sacramento, CA 95814
916/445-0834

Manager
Dept. of Education
Critical Health Initiatives
P.O. Box 944272-2720
Sacramento, CA 94244-2720
916/322-4018

Colorado

Legislative Council
State Capitol, Rm. 029
200 E. Colfax Ave.
Denver, CO 80203
303/866-3521

Project Director
Communities for a Drug-Free Colorado
140 E. 19th Ave., Suite 100
Denver, CO 80203
303/894-2750

Alcohol & Drug Abuse Div.
Dept. of Health
4210 E. 11th Ave.
Denver, CO 80220
303/331-8201

Dept. of Education
High Risk Intervention
201 E. Colfax Ave.
Denver, CO 80203
303/866-6766

Connecticut

Office of Legislative Research
Legislative Office Bldg.
18-20 Trinity St.
Hartford, CT 06106
203/566-8400

Chairman
Alcohol & Drug Abuse Commission
999 Asylum Ave.
Hartford, CT 06105
203/566-4145

Drug Abuse Preventiion Consultant
Dept. of Education
P.O. Box 2219
Hartford, CT 06145
203/566-2931

Delaware

Legislative Council
Legislative Hall
Legislative Ave.
P.O. Box 1401
Dover, DE 19903
302/736-4114

Chairman
Drug Abuse Coordinating Council
Elbert N. Carvel State Office Bldg.
820 N. French St.
Wilmington, DE 19801
302/571-3017

Bureau of Alcoholism & Drug Abuse
CT Bldg., Delaware State Hospital
1901 N. DuPont Hwy.
New Castle, DE 19720
302/421-6101

State Supervisor
Dept. of Public Instruction, Health
    Education, & Services
Townsend Bldg.
P.O. Box 1402
Dover, DE 19903
302/736-4886

District of Columbia

Office of Intergovernmental Relations
Executive Office of the Mayor
District Bldg., Rm. 416
1350 Pennsylvania Ave. NW
Washington, D.C. 20004
202/727-6265

Director: Drug Abuse Programs
District of Columbia
1111 E St. NW, Suite 500E
Washington, D.C. 20004
202/727-9472

Alcohol & Drug Abuse Services
　Administration
Universal North Bldg., Rm. 837
1875 Connecticut Ave. NW
Washington, D.C. 20009
202/673-6759

Director
Substance Abuse Program
D.C. Public Schools
Lovejoy Administrative Unit
12th & D Streets NE, Rm. 102
Washington, D.C. 20002
202/724-3610

Florida

Div. of Legislative Library Services
Joint Legislative Management Committee
State Legislature
The Capitol, Rm. 701
Tallahassee, FL 32399
904/488-2812

Chairman
Drug Policy Task Force
Executive Office of the Governor
2106 Capitol
Tallahassee, FL 32399-0001
904/488-1363

Alcohol & Drug Abuse Program
Bldg. 6, Rm. 156
1317 Winewood Blvd.
Tallahassee, FL 32399-0700
904/484-0900

Director
Prevention Center
Dept. of Education
325 W. Gaines St., Suite 414
Tallahassee, FL 32399-0400
904/488-6304

Georgia

Legislative Counsel
State Capitol, Rm. 316
Atlanta, GA 30334
404/656-5000

Deputy Director for Substance
　Abuse Services
Dept. of Human Resources
878 Peachtree St. NE, Suite 319
Atlanta, GA 30309
404/894-4200

Coordinator
Board of Education
Health & Physical Education
1952 Twin Towers E
Atlanta, GA 30334-5040
404/656-2414

Hawaii

Office of the Legislative Reference Bureau
State Capitol
415 S. Beretania St.
Honolulu, HI 96813
808/548-6237

State Drug Program Coordinator
P.O. Box 3044
Honolulu, HI 96802
808/548-2272

Drug Control Program
Office of Narcotics Enforcement
1100 Ward Ave., Suite 875
Honolulu, HI 96814
808/548-7186

Assistant Superintendent
Dept. of Education
P.O. Box 2360
Honolulu, HI 96804
808/548-2360

Idaho

Legislative Council
State Capitol Bldg.
700 W. Jefferson St.
Boise, ID 83720
208/334-2475

Bureau of Social Services
Dept. of Health & Welfare
Towers Bldg., 7th Floor
450 W. State St.
Boise, ID 83720
208/334-4085

Drug Education Consultant
Dept. of Education
Len B. Jordan Bldg.
Boise, ID 83720
208/334-2165

Illinois

Legislative Research Unit
222 S. College St.
3rd Floor, Suite A
Springfield, IL 62704
217/782-6851

Director
Dept. of Alcohol & Substance Abuse
222 S. College St., 2nd Floor
Springfield, IL 62704
217/782-0685

Dept. of Alcoholism & Substance Abuse
State of Illinois Center, Rm. 5-600
100 W. Randolph St.
Chicago, IL 60601
312/814-3840

Board of Education
Program Support Office
100 N. 1st St.
Springfield, IL 62777
217/782-3810

Indiana

Legislative Services Agency
State House, Rm. 302
200 W. Washington St.
Indianapolis, IN 46204
317/232-9550

Chairman
Governor's Commission on a Drug-Free
  Indiana
c/o Office of the Governor
State House
200 W. Washington St.
Indianapolis, IN 46204
317/232-2588

Div. of Addiction Services
Dept. of Mental Health
117 E. Washington St.
Indianapolis, IN 46204-3647
317/232-7816

Dept. of Education
Center for School Improvement
State House, Rm. 229
Indianapolis, IN 46204-2798
317/232-6984

Iowa

Legislative Service Bureau
State Capitol Bldg.
Des Moines, IA 50319
515/281-3566

Coordinator
Governor's Alliance on Substance Abuse
Lucas State Office Bldg., 2nd Floor
321 E. 12th St.
Des Moines, IA 50319
515/281-3784

Substance Abuse Division
Lucas State Office Bldg., 4th Floor
321 E. 12th St.
Des Moines, IA 50319
515/281-3641

Substance Education Consultant
Dept. of Education
Grimes State Office Bldg.
Des Moines, IA 50319
515/281-3021

Kansas

Legislative Research Dept.
State House, Rm. 545-N
Topeka, KS 66612
913/296-3181

Special Assistant on Drug Abuse
Governor's Office of Drug Abuse Programs
State House, Rm. 265-E
Topeka, KS 66612-1572
913/296-2584

Alcohol & Drug Abuse Services
Dept. of Social & Rehabilitation Services
Biddle Bldg., 2nd Floor
2700 W. 6th St.
Topeka, KS 66606
913/296-3925

Program Specialist
Substance Abuse
Dept. of Education
120 E. 10th St.
Topeka, KS 66612
913/296-4946

Kentucky

Legislative Research Commission
State Capitol Bldg.
Frankfort, KY 40601
502/564-8100

Executive Director
Champions Against Drugs
612-B Shelby St.
Frankfurt, KY 40601
502/564-7889

Div. of Substance Abuse
Dept. of Mental Health & Mental
  Retardation
Cabinet for Human Resources
Health Services Bldg.
275 E. Main St.
Frankfort, KY 40601
502/564-2880

Branch Manager
Dept. of Education
Alcohol/Drug Unit
1720 Capitol Plaza Tower
Frankfort, KY 40601
502/564-6720

Louisiana

Legislative Services
House of Representatives
State Capitol
900 Riverside N
P.O. Box 44486
Baton Rouge, LA 70804
504/342-7393

Liaison to Coordinating Council
Office of the Governor
P.O. Box 94004
Baton Rouge, LA 70804-9004
504/342-7015

Prevention & Recovery from Alcohol
  & Drug Abuse Office
Dept. of Health & Human Resources
2744-B Wooddale Blvd.
P.O. Box 53219
Baton Rouge, LA 70892
504/922-0730

Director
Bureau of Student Services
Dept. of Education
P.O. Box 94064
Baton Rouge, LA 70804-9064
504/342-3388

Maine

Revisor of Statutes Office
State House, Station 7, Rm. 108
Augusta, ME 04333
207/289-1650

Director
Office of Alcohol & Drug Abuse Prevention
State House, Station 11
Augusta, ME 04333
207/289-2781

Program Resources Coordinator
Dept. of Education & Cultural Services
Stevens School Complex
State House, Station 57
Augusta, ME 04333
207/289-3876

Maryland

Dept. of Legislative Reference
Legislative Services Bldg.
90 State Circle
Annapolis, MD 21401
301/841-3865

Chairman
Governor's Drug & Alcohol Abuse
  Commission
State House
Annapolis, MD 21401
301/974-3077

Drug Abuse Administration
Dept. of Health & Mental Hygiene
Herbert R. O'Conor State Office Bldg.
201 W. Preston St.
Baltimore, MD 21201
301/225-6925

Director
Dept. of Education
Drug-Free Schools Program
200 W. Baltimore St.
Baltimore, MD 21201
301/333-2324

Massachusetts

Legislative Research Bureau
30 Winter St., 11th Floor
Boston, MA 02108
617/722-2345

Executive Director
Governor's Alliance Against Drugs
One Ashburton Pl., Rm. 2131
Boston, MA 02108
617/727-0786

Div. of Alcoholism & Drug Rehabilitation
Dept. of Public Health
150 Tremont St.
Boston, MA 02111
617/727-8614

Michigan

Legislative Service Bureau
Legislative Council
Billie Farnum Bldg., 3rd Floor
125 W. Allegany St.
P.O. Box 30036
Lansing, MI 48909
517/373-0170

Director
Office of Drug Agencies
Grandview Plaza
206 E. Michigan Ave.
P.O. Box 30026
Lansing, MI 48909
517/373-4700

Office of Substance Abuse Services
Dept. of Public Health
3500 N. Logan St.
P.O. Box 30035
Lansing, MI 48909
517/335-8810

Health Education Specialist
Comprehensive School Health Unit
Dept. of Education
P.O. Box 30008
Lansing, MI 48909
517/373-2589

Minnesota

Legislative Reference Library
State Office Bldg., Rm. 645
550 Cedar St.
St. Paul, MN 55155
612/296-3398

Director
Office of Drug Policy
Dept. of Public Safety
Transportation Bldg., Rm. 211
John Ireland Blvd.
St. Paul, MN 55155
612/296-1057

Chemical Dependency Program Div.
Dept. of Human Services
Space Center Bldg.
444 Lafayette Rd.
St. Paul, MN 55155
612/296-3991

Supervisor
Drug Abuse Program
Dept. of Education
Learner Support Systems
994 Capitol Square Bldg.
St. Paul, MN 55101
612/296-3925

Mississippi

Legislative Reference Bureau
P.O. Box 1018
Jackson, MS 39205
601/359-3135

Executive Director
Substance Abuse Policy Council
P.O. Box 220
Jackson, MS 39205-0220
601/359-3692

Div. of Alcohol & Drug Abuse
Dept. of Mental Health
1500 Woolfolk Rd.
Jackson, MS 39201
601/359-1297

Coordinator
Dept. of Education
550 High St.
Jackson, MS 39205
601/359-3598

Missouri

Committee on Legislative Research
State Capitol, Rm. 117A
Jefferson City, MO 65101
314/751-4223

Interagency Working Group for Drug
 & Alcohol Abuse
P.O. Box 720
Jefferson City, MO 65102
314/751-3222

Div. of Alcohol & Drug Abuse
Dept. of Mental Health
1915 Southridge
P.O. Box 687
Jefferson City, MO 65102
314/751-4942

Commissioner
Dept. of Elementary & Secondary
 Education
P.O. Box 480
Jefferson City, MO 65102
314/751-4234

Montana

Legislative Council
Capitol Bldg., Rm. 138
Helena, MT 59620
406/444-3064

Administrator of Crime Control
Scott Hart Bldg., Rm. 463
303 N. Roberts
Helena, MT 59620
406/444-3604

Alcohol & Drug Abuse Div.
Dept. of Institutions
1539 11th Ave.
Helena, MT 59620
406/444-2827

Drug-Free Coordinator
Dept. of Education
Office of Public Instruction
Capitol Bldg.
Helena, MT 59620
406/444-4434

Nebraska

Legislative Council
State Capitol, 7th Floor
1445 K St.
Lincoln, NE 68509
402/471-2221

Coordinator
Toward a Drug-Free Nebraska
P.O. Box 94601
Lincoln, NE 68509
402/471-2414

Div. of Alcoholism & Drug Abuse
Dept. of Public Institutions
Lincoln Regional Center Campus
W. Van Dorn & Folsom Streets
Lincoln, NE 68509
402/471-2851

Administrator of Curriculum
Dept. of Education
P.O. Box 94987
301 Centennial Mall S
Lincoln, NE 68509-4987
402/471-4332

Nevada

Legislative Counsel Bureau
Legislative Bldg., Rm. 148
401 S. Carson St.
Carson City, NV 89710
702/885-5668

Coordinator of Drug & Alcohol Programs
State of Nevada
Las Vegas, NV 89158
702/486-4181

Bureau of Alcohol & Drug Abuse
Dept. of Human Resources
Kinkead Bldg.
505 E. King St.
Carson City, NV 89710
702/885-4790

Deputy Superintendent
Dept. of Education
Office of Public Instruction
Capitol Complex
Carson City, NV 89710
702/885-3100

New Hampshire

Office of Legislative Services
State House, Rm. 109
107 N. Main St.
Concord, NH 03301
603/271-3435

Office of Alcohol & Drug Abuse Prevention
Dept. of Health & Human Services
Health & Human Services Bldg.
6 Hazen Dr.
Concord, NH 03301-6525
800/852-3345

Dept. of Education
State Office Park S
101 Pleasant St.
Concord, NH 03301
603/271-2632

New Jersey

Office of Legislative Services
State House Annex
CN 068
Trenton, NJ 08625
609/292-4661

Chairman
Governor's Coordinating Council
c/o Dept. of Alcoholism
129 E. Hanover St.
Trenton, NJ 08608
609/292-8949

Dept. of Health
129 E. Hanover St.
Trenton, NJ 08608
609/292-5760

Manager
Dept. of Education
General Academic Education
225 W. State St., CN 500
Trenton, NJ 08625
609/292-5780

New Mexico

Legislative Council Service
State Capitol, Rm. 334
Santa Fe, NM 87503
505/984-9600

Cabinet Secretary
Dept. of Public Safety
Drug Policy Board
P.O. Box 1628
Santa Fe, NM 87504-1628
505/827-3370

Drug Abuse Bureau
Health & Environment Dept.
Harold Runnels Bldg.
1190 St. Francis Dr.
Santa Fe, NM 87504-0968
505/827-2589

Drug-Free Schools Coordinator
Dept. of Education
300 Don Gaspar Ave.
Santa Fe, NM 87501
505/827-6648

New York

Legislative Library
State Capitol, Rm. 337
Albany, NY 12224
518/463-5683

Chairman
Governor's Anti-Drug Abuse Council
State Capitol, Rm. 326
Albany, NY 12224
518/474-4623

Div. of Substance Abuse Services
Office of Alcoholism & Substance Abuse
Executive Park S, 2nd Floor
Stuyvesant Plaza
Albany, NY 12203
518/457-2061

Chief
Dept. of Education
Bureau of Health & Drug Education
Washington Ave.
Albany, NY 12234
518/474-1491

North Carolina

Legislative Administration Officer
General Assembly
Dobbs Bldg., Rm. 1072
430 N. Salisbury St.
Raleigh, NC 27687
919/733-4000

Drug Cabinet
116 W. Jones St., Rm. G068
Raleigh, NC 27603-8006
919/733-5002

Alcohol & Drug Abuse Services Section
Div. of Mental Health, Mental Retarda-
    tion, & Substance Abuse Services
Dept. of Human Resources
Albermarle Bldg., Rm. 1124
325 N. Salisbury St.
Raleigh, NC 27611
919/733-4670

Director
Dept. of Public Instruction
Div. of Alcohol & Drug Defense
210 N. Dawson St.
Raleigh, NC 27603-1712
919/733-6615

North Dakota

Legislative Council
State Capitol
Bismarck, ND 58505
701/224-2916

Administrative Assistant
Office of the Governor
600 East Blvd.
State Capitol
Bismarck, ND 58505
701/224-2200

Div. of Alcoholism & Drug Abuse
Dept. of Human Services
State Capitol, Judicial Wing
Bismarck, ND 58505
701/224-2769

Director
Dept. of Public Instruction
Guidance/Drug-Free Schools
State Capitol, 9th Floor
Bismarck, ND 58505-0440
701/224-2269

Ohio

Legislative Service Commission
State House
Broad & High Streets
Columbus, OH 43215
614/466-3615

Director
Governor's Office of Alcohol & Drug
    Recovery Systems
170 N. High St., 3rd Floor
Columbus, OH 43215
614/644-7231

Bureau of Drug Abuse
Div. of Mental Health
170 N. High St., 3rd Floor
Columbus, OH 43215
614/466-7893

Assistant Director: Dept. of Education
Div. of Education Services
65 S. Front St., Rm. 719
Columbus, OH 43266-0308
614/466-3708

Oklahoma

Chairman
Drug Policy Board
State Capitol, Rm. 112
Oklahoma City, OK 73105
405/521-3921

Alcohol & Drug Abuse Programs
Programs Div.
P.O. Box 53277
Oklahoma City, OK 73152
405/521-0044

Director
Office of Federal Financially
    Assisted Programs
Dept. of Education
2500 N. Lincoln Blvd.
Oklahoma City, OK 73105-4599
405/521-2106

Oregon

Legislative Research
Legislative Administration Committee
State Capitol, Rm. S420
Salem, OR 97310
503/378-8871

Assistant Director
Office of Alcohol & Drug Abuse
    Programs
Dept. of Human Resources
1178 Cherneketa St. NE
Salem, OR 97310
503/378-2163

Associate Superintendent
Dept. of Education
Div. of Special Student Services
700 Pringle Pkwy. SE
Salem, OR 97310
503/378-2677

Pennsylvania

Legislative Reference Bureau
Main Capitol Bldg., Rm. 641
Harrisburg, PA 17120
717/787-5323

Executive Director
Drug Policy Council
Executive Office of the Governor
Finance Bldg., Rm. 310
Harrisburg, PA 17120
717/783-8626

Office of Drug & Alcohol Programs
Dept. of Health
Health & Welfare Bldg., Rm. 809
Forster St. & Commonwealth Ave.
Harrisburg, PA 17108
717/787-9857

Drug-Free Schools Coordinator
Div. of Student Services
Dept. of Education
333 Market St.
Harrisburg, PA 17126-0333
717/783-9294

Rhode Island

Legislative Council
State House, Rm. 101
82 Smith St.
Providence, RI 02909
401/277-3757

Director of Drug Programs
Office of the Governor
State House
82 Smith St.
Providence, RI 02903
401/277-1290

Div. of Substance Abuse
Dept. of Mental Health, Retardation,
   & Hospitals
Substance Abuse Administration Bldg.
Cranston, RI 02920
401/464-2091

Director
Dept. of Education
School Support Services
22 Hayes St.
Providence, RI 02908
401/277-2638

South Carolina

Code Commissioner & Director
Legislative Council
State House
Columbia, SC 29211
803/734-2145

State Drug Program Coordinator
South Carolina Law Enforcement Div.
P.O. Box 21398
Columbia, SC 29221
803/737-9051

Commission on Alcohol & Drug Abuse
3700 Forest Dr., Suite 300
Columbia, SC 29204
803/734-9542

Dept. of Education
At-Risk Youth Program
1429 Senate St., Rm. 1206
Columbia, SC 29201
803/734-8097

South Dakota

Legislative Research Council
State Capitol Annex
500 E. Capitol Ave.
Pierre, SD 57501
605/773-3251

Special Assistant for Human Resources
Office of the Governor
Pierre, SD 57501
605/773-3212

Div. of Alcohol & Drug Abuse
Dept. of Health
Joe Foss Bldg.
523 E. Capitol Ave.
Pierre, SD 57501-3182
605/773-3123

Drug-Free Schools Director
Dept. of Education
Div. of Education
700 Governor's Dr.
Pierre, SD 57501-2291
605/773-4670

Tennessee

Office of Legislative Services
General Assembly
State Capitol, Rm. G3
Nashville, TN 37219
615/741-3511

Coordinator
Drug-Free Tennessee
c/o Governor's Planning Office
309 John Sevier Bldg.
Nashville, TN 37219
615/741-1676

Div. of Alcohol & Drug Abuse Services
Dept. of Mental Health & Mental
  Retardation
James K. Polk State Office Bldg.
4th Floor
505 Deaderick St.
Nashville, TN 37219
615/741-1921

Coordinator
Dept. of Education
Drug-Free Schools Program
140 Cordell Hull Bldg.
Nashville, TN 37219
615/741-6055

Texas

Legislative Council
State Capitol, Rm. 155
Congress Ave.
Austin, TX 78711
512/463-1151

General Counsel
State of Texas
P.O. Box 12428
Austin, TX 78711
512/463-1988

Commission on Alcohol & Drug Abuse
1705 Guadalupe St.
Austin, TX 78701
512/463-5510

Drug-Free Schools Coordinator
Texas Education Agency
Drug Abuse Prevention Program
1701 N. Congress Ave., Rm. 5-123
Austin, TX 78701-1494
512/463-9501

Utah

Office of Legislative Research
  & General Counsel
State Capitol, Rm. 436
Salt Lake City, UT 84114
801/533-5481

Commission on Criminal & Juvenile Justice
101 State Capitol
Salt Lake City, UT 84114
801/538-1031

Div. of Alcoholism & Drugs
Dept. of Social Services
Social Services Bldg.
150 W. North Temple St.
Salt Lake City, UT 84145-0500
801/533-6532

Educational Specialist
Office of Education
Drug-Free Schools Program
250 East 500 S
Salt Lake City, UT 84111
801/538-7713

Vermont

Legislative Council
State House
115 State St.
Montpelier, VT 05602
802/828-2231

State Drug Program Coordinator
Director of State Police
Waterbury, VT 05676
802/244-7345

Office of Alcohol & Drug Abuse Programs
Agency of Human Services
Waterbury Office Complex
Building 1 N
103 S. Main St.
Waterbury, VT 05676
802/241-2170

Dept. of Education
Drug-Free Schools Program
120 State St.
Montpelier, VT 05602-2703
802/828-3111

Virginia

Div. of Legislative Services
General Assembly Bldg.
910 Capitol St.
Richmond, VA 23208
804/786-3591

State Drug Program Coordinator
Dept. of Health & Human Resources
P.O. Box 1475
Richmond, VA 23212
804/786-7765

Office of Substance Abuse Services
Dept. of Mental Health & Mental
    Retardation
Madison Bldg.
109 Governor St.
Richmond, VA 23214
804/786-3906

Supervisor
Dept. of Education
Health & Physical Education
P.O. Box 6-Q
Richmond, VA 23216-2060
804/225-2733

Washington

Office of Program Research
House of Representatives
House Office Bldg., Rm. 230
Olympia, WA 98504
206/786-7102

Special Assistant on Drug Issues
Insurance Bldg., 4th Floor
Mail Stop AQ-44
Olympia, WA 98504
206/586-0827

Bureau of Alcohol & Substance Abuse
Office Bldg. 2
12th Ave. & Franklin St.
Olympia, WA 98504
206/753-5866

Supervisor
Dept. of Public Instruction
Substance Abuse Education
Old Capitol Bldg., FG-11
Olympia, WA 98504
206/753-5595

West Virginia

Legislative Services
State Capitol, Rm. E-132
Charleston, WV 25305
304/348-2040

State Drug Program Coordinator
Secretary
Dept. of Public Safety
P.O. Box 2930
State Capitol Complex
Charleston, WV 25305
304/348-2930

Div. on Alcoholism & Drug Abuse
State Office Bldg. 3, Rm. 451
1800 Washington St. E
Charleston, WV 25305
304/348-2276

Coordinator of Drug Education
Dept. of Education
Student Support Services
Capitol Complex, B-309
Charleston, WV 25305
304/348-8830

Wisconsin

Legislative Reference Bureau
State Capitol, Rm. 201N
Madison, WI 53702
608/266-0361

Coordinator
State Alliance for a Drug-Free Wisconsin
Madison, WI 53702
608/266-9923

Office of Alcohol & Drug Abuse
Wilson St. State Office Bldg., Rm. 434
One W. Wilson St.
Madison, WI 53707
608/266-2717

Chief, Programs Development
Dept. of Public Instruction
Bureau for Pupil Services
125 S. Webster St.
Madison, WI 53707
608/266-0963

Wyoming

Legislative Service Office
State Capitol, Rm. 213
200 W. 24th St.
Cheyenne, WY 82002
307/777-7881

Chairman
Governor's State Drug Policy Board
316 W. 22nd St.
Cheyenne, WY 82002-0001
307/777-7181

Office of Substance Abuse Programs
Hathaway Bldg., Rm. 350
2300 Capitol Ave.
Cheyenne, WY 82002
307/777-7115

Coordinator
Dept. of Education
Office of Public Instruction
Hathaway Bldg.
2300 Capitol Ave.
Cheyenne, WY 82002
307/777-6202

FEDERAL GOVERNMENT AGENCIES

Executive Office of the President

Office of National Drug Control Policy
Executive Office of the President
Washington, D.C. 20500
202/673-2823

U.S. Department of Health and Human Services

Centers for Disease Control
Office on Smoking and Health
Parklawn Bldg., Rm. 116
5600 Fishers Lane
Rockville, MD 20857
301/443-5287

National Cancer Institute
Office of Cancer Communication
National Institutes of Health
Bldg. 31, Rm. 10A-24
9000 Rockville Pike
Bethesda, MD 20892
800/422-6237

National Clearinghouse for Alcohol
  & Drug Information
6000 Executive Blvd.
P.O. Box 2345
Rockville, MD 20852
301/468-2600

National Health Information Center
1010 Wayne Ave., Suite 300
Silver Spring, MD 20910
800/336-4797
301/565-4167 in Maryland

National Heart, Lung, & Blood Institute
National Institutes of Health
9000 Rockville Pike
Bethesda, MD 20892
301/496-4236

National Institute on Alcoholism
  & Alcohol Abuse
5600 Fishers Lane, Rm. 14C-17
P.O. Box 2345
Rockville, MD 20857
301/443-2954

National Institute on Drug Abuse
Parklawn Bldg.
5600 Fishers Lane
Rockville, MD 20857
301/443-6245

National Institute of Mental Health
5600 Fishers Lane, Rm. 15C-05
Rockville, MD 20857
301/443-3414

Office of Substance Abuse Prevention
Parklawn Bldg.
5600 Fishers Lane
Rockville, MD 20857
301/443-0365

Surgeon General
U.S. Public Health Service
200 Independence Ave. SW
Washington, D.C. 20201
202/245-6467

U.S. Department of the Treasury

United States Customs Service
1301 Constitution Ave. NW, Rm. 611
Washington, D.C. 20229
202/566-8195

U.S. Department of Education

Alcohol & Drug Abuse Education Program
Drug-Free Schools Staff
400 Maryland Ave. SW, Rm. 2135
Washington, D.C. 20202-6439
202/732-4599

U.S. Department of Housing and Urban Development

Office for Drug-Free Neighborhoods
451 7th St. SW
Washington, D.C. 20241
202/755-7197

Drug Information and Strategy
   Clearinghouse
P.O. Box 6424
Rockville, MD 20850
800/245-2691

U.S. Department of Justice

Drug Enforcement Administration
Demand Reduction Section
600 Army Navy Drive
Arlington, VA 20537
202/307-7977

Drug & Alcohol Abuse Prevention
   & Treatment Section
Office of Juvenile Justice
   & Delinquency Prevention
633 Indiana Ave. NW, Rm. 758
Washington, D.C. 20531
202/307-5914

Drugs & Crime Data Center
   & Clearinghouse
1600 Research Blvd.
Rockville, MD 20850
800/666-3332

National School Safety Center
Office of Juvenile Justice
   & Delinquency Prevention
16830 Ventura Blvd., Suite 200
Encino, CA 91436
818/377-6200

Safe School Program
National Institute of Justice
633 Indiana Ave. NW, Rm. 805
Washington, D.C. 20531
202/272-6040

U.S. Department of State

Bureau of International Narcotics Matters
2201 C St. NW, Rm. 7331
Washington, D.C. 20520
202/647-6642

DRUG-FREE SCHOOLS & COMMUNITIES REGIONAL CENTERS

Regional Centers

Northeast Regional Center for Drug-Free Schools and Communities
12 Overton Ave.
Sayville, NY 11782-0403
516/589-7022

Southeast Regional Center for Drug-Free Schools and Communities
The Hurt Bldg., Suite 210
50 Hurt Plaza
Atlanta, GA 30303
404/688-9227

Midwest Regional Center for Drug-Free Schools and Communities
2001 N. Clybourn, Suite 302
Chicago, IL 60614
312/883-8888

Southwest Regional Center for Drug-Free Schools and Communities
555 Constitution Ave.
Norman, OK 73037
405/325-1454
800/234-7972 (outside Oklahoma)

Western Regional Center for Drug-Free Schools and Communities
101 S.W. Main St., Suite 500
Portland, OR 97204
503/275-9479
800/547-6339 (outside Oregon)

States Served

Connecticut, Delaware, Maine, Maryland, Massachusetts, New Hampshire, New Jersey, New York Ohio, Pennsylvania, Rhode Island Vermont

Alabama, District of Columbia, Florida, Georgia, Kentucky, North Carolina, South Carolina Tennessee, Virginia, West Virginia, Virgin Islands, Puerto Rico

Indiana, Illinois, Iowa, Michigan, Minnesota, Missouri, Nebraska, North Dakota, South Dakota, Wisconsin

Arizona, Arkansas, Colorado, Kansas, Louisiana, Mississippi, New Mexico, Oklahoma, Texas, Utah

Alaska, California, Hawaii, Idaho, Montana, Nevada, Oregon, Washington, Wyoming, American Samoa, Guam

CANADIAN RESOURCES

Addiction Research Foundation
Health and Welfare, Canada
33 Russell St.
Toronto, ON M5F 2S1
CANADA
416/595-6000

Canadian Cancer Society
77 Bloor St. W, Suite 1702
Toronto, ON M5S 3A1
CANADA
416/961-7223

Canadian Lung Association
75 Albert St., Suite 908
Ottawa, ON K1T 5E7
CANADA
613/237-1208

Counsel on Drug Abuse
698 Weston Rd.
Toronto, ON M6N 3R3
CANADA
416/763-1491

Concerns, Canada
11 Progress Ave., Suite 200
Scarborough, ON M1P 4S7
CANADA
416/293-3400

Canadian Heart Foundation
1 Nicholas St., Suite 1200
Ottawa, ON K1N 7B7
CANADA
613/237-4361

Heart and Stroke Foundation
  of Canada
160 George St., Suite 200
Ottawa, ON K1N 9M2
CANADA
613/237-4361

Public Health Branch
5th Floor, 15 Overlea Blvd.
Toronto, ON M4H 1A9
CANADA
414-392-2437

Health Information (National Government)
9th Floor, Hepburn Block
Queen's Park
Toronto, ON M7A 1S2
CANADA
416/965-3101
800/268-1153